MANDALA MAGIC

Amazing Mandalas to Color

BARRON'S

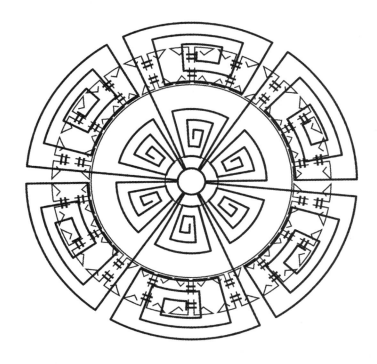

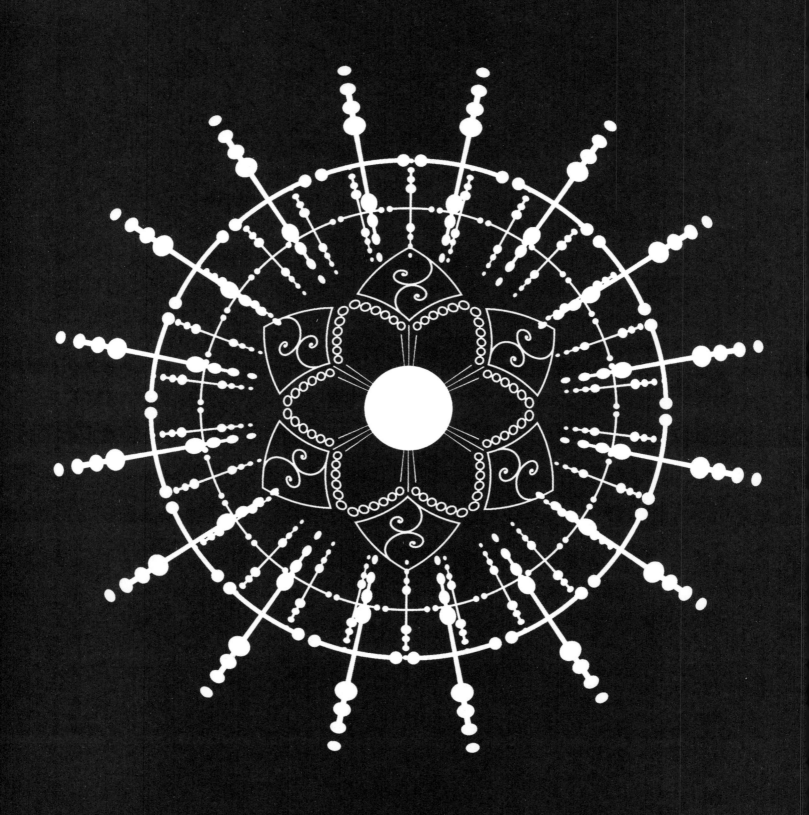

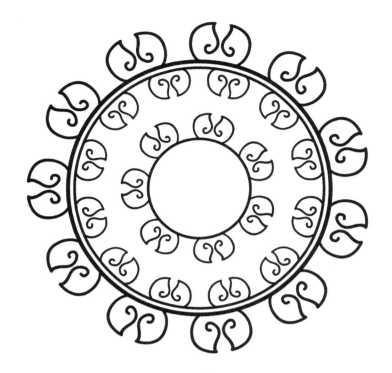

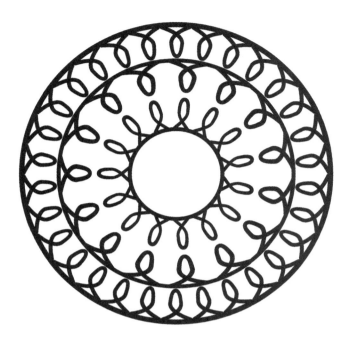

First edition for the United States, its territories
and dependencies, and Canada published in 2015
by Barron's Educational Series, Inc.

Original German title: *Mandala-Zauber:*
Fantastisches zum Ausmalen
© Copyright 2015 by arsEdition GmbH, München

All inquiries should be addressed to:
Barron's Educational Series, Inc.
250 Wireless Boulevard
Hauppauge, NY 11788
www.barronseduc.com

ISBN: 978-1-4380-0638-3

Production: Grafisches Atelier, arsEdition
Illustrations: Grafisches Atelier, Luisa Amann, Lea John, Nora John

Printed in Canada
9 8

For best results, colored pencils are recommended.